LITTLE BOOK OF
MOCKTAILS

Rufus Cavendish

summersdale

THE LITTLE BOOK OF MOCKTAILS

Text by Anna Lou Walker

An Hachette UK Company
www.hachette.co.uk

Summersdale Publishers Ltd
Part of Octopus Publishing Group Limited
Carmelite House
50 Victoria Embankment
LONDON
EC4Y 0DZ
UK

www.summersdale.com

Printed and bound in Poland

ISBN: 978-1-80007-150-6

Substantial discounts on bulk quantities of Summersdale books are available to corporations, professional associations and other organizations. For details contact general enquiries: telephone: +44 (0) 1243 771107 or email: enquiries@summersdale.com.

CONTENTS

INTRODUCTION

There's never been a better time to master the mocktail. Challenges such as Dry January have exploded in popularity and more and more people are looking to enjoy alcohol-free drinks all year round. Perhaps you're cutting down for health reasons, because you're tired of morning-after headaches, you're looking to save money or you simply want to try something new. Not drinking booze doesn't have to mean sipping chaste glasses of water at every social function, however. Mocktails are more sophisticated than ever before, and our recipes for alcohol-free drinking will give you all the inspiration you need to wow at your next party. Mocktails are soft drinks with flare. Your non-alcoholic tipple can be fruity, tart, botanical or wonderfully sweet: there's a recipe to suit every taste, and a creative garnish or mixology technique to entertain even the most sour-faced guest.

The

ESSENTIALS

THE EQUIPMENT

Cocktail shaker

Perhaps the most important item in your mocktail-making armoury. Not only are cocktail shakers crucial for seamlessly combining your ingredients, but they're also a cornerstone of cocktail party culture. No good bartender is without their signature shake, so make sure you practise before hosting! There are a variety of styles on the market, including French, Boston and cobbler.

Strainer

Certain mocktails must be strained in order to achieve a smooth texture and filter out pulp. Cocktail strainers are easy to find in stores, or simply repurpose your tea strainer.

Bar spoon

These long-handled metal spoons are ideal for stirring tall drinks without getting your fingers wet.

Muddler

Muddlers are chunky rods with flat, ridged ends, used for crushing together solid ingredients. You can easily fashion a muddler from things already in your kitchen, such as the end of a rolling pin or a pestle.

Punch bowl

A stylish punch bowl can make for the centrepiece of your mocktail party. Bonus points for a matching ladle!

Lemon squeezer

Available in a host of creative designs and styles, these are the best way to get maximum juice from your citrus fruits.

Blender

Enjoy crushed ice mocktails such as the Daiquiri? A blender allows you to combine ice and solid fruit for a thick, smoothie-like texture.

THE TECHNIQUES

Muddle

Muddling is the act of crushing solid ingredients together
in a glass to allow the flavours to infuse – for example,
sugar, mint and lime for a Mojito (or No-jito!). Press your
muddler firmly into the ingredients with a grinding action
to release the flavours.

Stir

This gentle method of combining ingredients avoids
getting unnecessary bubbles into the texture of the
mocktail. Slowly stir using your bar spoon until all
ingredients are combined.

Strain

Crucial for mocktail recipes with solid ingredients (such
as lime). Straining your mix into the glass offers a finer
final texture.

Shake

Place your ice and ingredients in a shaker, give the lid a good smack to ensure it is tightly closed and shake vigorously. When the shaker itself has become cold, your drink is usually ready (assuming you have added ice), but do check that it's fully combined before decanting.

TIPS FOR MOCKTAIL MAKING

1 Chill your glasses before serving. Almost every mocktail tastes better for being ice cold.

2 Use the correct glass for your mocktail. Each recipe page will indicate which glass best suits the drink.

poco grande   highball   short

martini   flute   margarita

3 Sample every mocktail before serving it up. Ingredients like fruit and juices can vary in their sweetness – give it a taste and adapt as necessary.

4 Make sure you have a variety of garnish options to hand. From fresh and dried fruit through to cocktail umbrellas and edible glitter, there are a host of options out there.

5 Get creative. You're already breaking the rules of traditional cocktail crafting by skipping the spirits, so adapt recipes however you like. You never know, you might just stumble on a signature mocktail of your own!

TIPS FOR HOSTING A MOCKTAIL PARTY

1 Preparation is everything! Mocktails can be fiddly, so before your guests arrive, ensure you either pre-make a punchbowl of your blend, or lay out your ingredients and tools in an area that is easy to access and kept tidy throughout the evening.

2 Stock up on ice. You'll be amazed how much you get through.

3 A party theme can be a great way to get guests excited – it's also a brilliant way to select your drinks menu. Feeling a tiki vibe? Tropical drinks are your go-to. More of a speakeasy feel? Martinis and Old Fashioneds are the order of the day.

4 Create a bespoke playlist. Select tracks that match your theme, or the mood you're hoping to create. Make sure it's a few hours long, and have it playing before your guests arrive.

The

MOCKTAILS

Classic

NADA - RITA

THE MARGARITA IS A CLASSIC IN THE COCKTAIL WORLD, AND FEW BARS WON'T BE ABLE TO SHAKE ONE UP ON DEMAND, EVEN IF IT DOESN'T FEATURE ON THE MENU. THESE ZINGY MEXICAN MIXES ARE A POPULAR PARTY DRINK, OFTEN SERVED BY THE PITCHER RATHER THAN THE GLASS. HAPPILY FOR MOCKTAIL LOVERS, THEY'RE JUST AS DELICIOUS AS VIRGIN "NADA-RITAS".

Stir

DIFFICULTY: 🍷   **GLASS TYPE:** 🍸

REQUIRED: 1 LIME, SMALL PLATE OF SEA SALT,
ICE CUBES, 3 TBSP FRESH LIME JUICE,
½ TSP HONEY, 30 ML SICILIAN LEMONADE

1 Prepare your lime by cutting it in half. One side should be halved again, the other sliced into rounds.

2 Run one of the lime quarters around the rim of your glass to coat it in juice. Sprinkle the sea salt onto a plate and dip the rim, so that it gains a light smattering of salt.

3 Add ice cubes, combine the other ingredients in the glass and gently stir.

4 Garnish with a lime round.

Blooming

MARY

THE BLOODY MARY IS OFTEN
TOTED AS THE ULTIMATE HANGOVER
CURE, BUT IF HAIR OF THE DOG
FEELS A LITTLE TOO INTENSE FOR
YOUR THROBBING HEAD, A VIRGIN
BLOOMING MARY MIGHT BE JUST THE
TICKET. WITH TOMATO JUICE, SPICES,
WORCESTERSHIRE SAUCE AND CELERY
IN THE MIX, IT'S DEFINITELY A
SAVOURY MOCKTAIL, AND THERE ARE
A HOST OF VARIATIONS AVAILABLE,
INCLUDING THE "SURF 'N' TURF
BLOOMING MARY", WHICH INCLUDES
GARNISHES OF SHRIMP AND BACON
ALONGSIDE THE TRADITIONAL CELERY.

Stir

DIFFICULTY: ❢ ❢   **GLASS TYPE:** ▌

REQUIRED: ICE CUBES, 100 ML TOMATO JUICE, JUICE OF 2 LEMONS, WORCESTERSHIRE SAUCE (TO TASTE), 1 CELERY STICK, A PINCH OF GROUND PEPPER AND CELERY SALT, HOT SAUCE (TO TASTE)

1 Fill your glass with ice and add the tomato juice, lemon juice and Worcestershire sauce, using the celery stick to gently stir.

2 Gradually add the pepper, salt and hot sauce and stir again, sampling to ensure the heat matches your taste.

3 Serve with the celery stick still in the glass.

MAI TAI... IT'S LIKE VACATION IN A GLASS!

KATIE LEE

my
TAI

THE MAI TAI IS A FRUITY, RUM-BASED COCKTAIL AND THE UNDISPUTED KING OF THE TROPICAL COCKTAIL WORLD. THE NAME IS TAKEN FROM THE TAHITIAN WORD *MAITA'I* MEANING "GOOD" OR "EXCELLENT", WHICH TRANSLATES BRILLIANTLY TO THE WORLD OF MOCKTAIL AS THE MY TAI. THOUGH MOST LIKELY FIRST DEVISED IN THE 1930s, THE MAI TAI STORMED THE COCKTAIL WORLD IN THE 1950s WITH THE RISING POPULARITY OF TIKI-THEMED BARS. ITS PROMINENT ROLE IN THE ELVIS PRESLEY MOVIE *BLUE HAWAII* CERTAINLY DIDN'T DULL ITS CHARM EITHER.

Shake

DIFFICULTY: 🍷 🍷   **GLASS TYPE:** ■

REQUIRED: 80 ML PINEAPPLE JUICE, 80 ML ORANGE JUICE, 80 ML SODA WATER, CRUSHED ICE, PINEAPPLE WEDGE

1. Combine the pineapple juice, orange juice, soda water and ice in a cocktail shaker and shake vigorously until cold.

2. Cut a slit halfway down the pineapple wedge and position it onto the rim of your glass.

3. Pour the cocktail into the glass without straining.

Calm Blue

LAGOON

THERE'S NO MISTAKING THE VIVID, ALMOST NEON SHADE OF THE BLUE LAGOON COCKTAIL. USUALLY SERVED LONG AND WITH A SHOWBOAT ARRAY OF GARNISHES, THIS DRINK COULD PASS AS A TABLE CENTREPIECE AS WELL AS A TIPPLE. THE SIGNATURE BLUE COLOUR CAN BE ACHIEVED IN A NUMBER OF WAYS. THOUGH FOOD COLOURING IS OFTEN THE SECRET TO THE HIGHLY CONCENTRATED HUE, FOR OUR CALM BLUE LAGOON RECIPE WE RECOMMEND BLUE CURAÇAO SYRUP, WHICH IS MADE FROM THE DRIED PEEL OF THE CARIBBEAN LARAHA CITRUS FRUIT. MAKE SURE YOU PURCHASE THE NON-ALCOHOLIC VARIETY.

Stir

DIFFICULTY: ▮

GLASS TYPE: ▮

REQUIRED: 2 TSP LEMON JUICE, SMALL HANDFUL OF MINT LEAVES, 2 TSP NON-ALCOHOLIC CURAÇAO SYRUP, 2 TSP SUGAR SYRUP, ICE CUBES, 200 ML SODA WATER, SLICE OF LEMON

1 Using a muddler, combine the lemon juice, mint leaves (leaving one aside for garnish) and syrups in the glass.

2 Add the ice and soda water and stir.

3 Garnish with a mint leaf and a slice of lemon.

I THINK THE NEGRONI IS THE PERFECT COCKTAIL... IT IS BOTH APERITIF AND DIGESTIVE. IT'S A RARE DRINK THAT CAN DO THAT.

ANTHONY BOURDAIN

NO - GRONI

THE ITALIAN NEGRONI IS ONE OF
THE MOST SOPHISTICATED DRINKS
ON A CLASSIC COCKTAIL MENU, BUT
DUE TO ITS HIGH ALCOHOL CONTENT
(GIN, VERMOUTH *AND* CAMPARI) IT
CAN BE DIFFICULT TO REPLICATE FOR A
VIRGIN COCKTAIL PARTY. THE KEY IS TO
SELECT NATURALLY RICH AND BITTER
FLAVOURS. THE TWIST OF ORANGE
PEEL IN OUR NO-GRONI RECIPE GIVES
THAT BITE OF BITTERNESS, WHILE THE
POMEGRANATE JUICE PROVIDES DEPTH
AND RICHNESS, ALONG WITH THAT
CLASSIC RUBY RED COLOUR.

Stir

DIFFICULTY: 🍷   **GLASS TYPE:** ■

REQUIRED: 200 ML POMEGRANATE JUICE, 2 TSP
CHERRY CONCENTRATE, ICE CUBES, PINCH
EACH OF NUTMEG, CINNAMON AND CLOVES,
ORANGE PEEL TO GARNISH

1   Combine the pomegranate juice and cherry
concentrate over ice in your glass.

2   Add the pinches of nutmeg, cinnamon and cloves,
adjusting to taste. Stir.

3   Twist the orange peel to release the bitter flavours,
garnish and enjoy.

Unicorn

JUICE

A MOCKTAIL DOESN'T HAVE TO IMITATE A CLASSIC COCKTAIL IN ORDER TO STEAL THE SHOW — THE COLOUR-CHANGING MAGIC OF UNICORN JUICE IS A SHOWSTOPPER IN ITS OWN RIGHT! THE KEY TO THIS DRINKABLE MAGIC TRICK IS IN THE ICE, WHICH WILL REQUIRE A BIT OF PRE-PARTY PLANNING. AS IT MELTS, THE COLOUR FROM THE PEA FLOWERS TURN THE MOCKTAIL A DEEP PURPLE HUE. GREAT FOR KIDS OR THE YOUNG AT HEART, IT'LL CERTAINLY PROVIDE A TALKING POINT FOR ANY PARTY, AND THE REFRESHING LEMONADE FLAVOURS ARE PERFECT FOR A SUMMER DAY.

Stir

DIFFICULTY: ♟ ♟ ♟ GLASS TYPE: ▮

REQUIRED: 7 BLUE BUTTERFLY PEA FLOWERS, 100 ML
BOILING WATER, JUICE OF 5 LEMONS, ZEST
OF 1 LEMON, 150 G SUGAR, 200 ML CLUB
SODA, SLICE OF LEMON

1 Add the blue pea flowers to boiling water and steep
until the liquid turns a deep blue. Strain the water,
allow it to cool, then freeze in an ice cube tray.
Once frozen, crush in a blender.

2 Combine the lemon juice, zest and sugar in a
saucepan to create the syrup. Heat and stir until
dissolved and thickened, then cool to allow the
colour to be fully released.

3 Fill $^1/_3$ glass with the crushed ice, another $^1/_3$ with
the lemon syrup, then top with club soda.

4 Garnish with a slice of lemon and enjoy.

I DON'T NEED A FANCY
PARTY TO BE HAPPY.
JUST GOOD FRIENDS, GOOD
FOOD, AND GOOD LAUGHS.

MARIA SHARAPOVA

Classic

NO-JITO

IS THERE ANY DRINK MORE
SYNONYMOUS WITH HOLIDAYS THAN
THE MOJITO? A REFRESHING LONG
GLASS OF LIME, SUGAR AND MINT
– THE COMBINATION OF SWEET AND
CITRUS IS UNMISTAKABLY SUMMERY.
IT WAS FIRST CREATED IN HAVANA,
CUBA, AND MANY HISTORIANS POINT
TO ENSLAVED AFRICAN PEOPLE
WORKING IN THE CUBAN SUGAR FIELDS
AS THE ORIGINATORS OF THE MOJITO'S
TASTE, THANKS TO THEIR LOVE FOR
THE SUGAR CANE JUICE THAT OFTEN
FORMS ITS BASE. THIS NO-JITO
OFFERS ALL THE REFRESHMENT
WITH NO NEXT-DAY HEADACHE.

Stir

DIFFICULTY: 🍷🍷   **GLASS TYPE:** ▮

REQUIRED: GENEROUS PINCH OF SUGAR, 2 WEDGES OF LIME, SMALL HANDFUL OF MINT LEAVES, ICE CUBES, 4 TBSP OF APPLE JUICE, 250 ML SODA WATER, JUICE OF 1 LIME

1 Place the sugar and a wedge of lime in the bottom of your glass and muddle. Smack the mint leaves against your palm to release the flavour, add half to the glass and muddle the mixture again.

2 Add ice and pour over the apple juice and soda water, then stir. Add lime juice to taste.

3 Use the rest of the mint leaves and another wedge of lime to garnish.

Snowy

RUSSIAN

FROM A SUMMER DRINK TO A QUINTESSENTIAL WINTER INDULGENCE — THE CREAMY WHITE RUSSIAN IS SURPRISINGLY NOT AT ALL RUSSIAN IN ORIGIN, BUT IS SO-CALLED BECAUSE VODKA IS THE KEY INGREDIENT IN ITS ALCOHOLIC FORM. THE DRINK EXPLODED IN POPULARITY AFTER BEING FEATURED IN THE 1998 FILM *THE BIG LEBOWSKI*, WHERE IT'S THE DRINK OF CHOICE FOR JEFFREY "THE DUDE" LEBOWSKI (THOUGH HE OFTEN REFERS TO IT AS A "CAUCASIAN" RATHER THAN ITS PROPER NAME). THIS SNOWY RUSSIAN MOCKTAIL IS A GREAT CHOICE FOR COFFEE LOVERS.

Shake

DIFFICULTY: 🍷   **GLASS TYPE:** ■

REQUIRED: ICE CUBES, 200 ML MILK (DAIRY
OR ALTERNATIVE), CHOCOLATE
SHAVINGS, DASH OF COFFEE SYRUP,
CINNAMON STICK

1 Place the ice, milk, chocolate and coffee syrup in
a cocktail shaker and shake vigorously.

2 Strain and garnish with cinnamon stick.

3 Drink immediately to avoid separation.

TO BE HONEST, I REALLY DO LOVE A COSMOPOLITAN.

SARAH JESSICA PARKER

Cheat's

COSMOPOLITAN

EVERY *SEX AND THE CITY* FAN KNOWS THAT THE COSMOPOLITAN IS THE DRINK OF CHOICE FOR CARRIE AND THE GIRLS, AND ITS FREQUENT APPEARANCE ON THE SHOW HAS GAINED THE COCKTAIL A REPUTATION SYNONYMOUS WITH NEW YORK'S MOST FASHIONABLE SOCIETY. HISTORIANS DISAGREE ABOUT THE ORIGINS OF THE COSMO — THOUGH CERTAINLY A MODERN TIPPLE, COMPETING ACCOUNTS SUGGEST IT WAS BORN IN EITHER THE GAY COMMUNITIES OF MASSACHUSETTS, A STEAK HOUSE IN MINNEAPOLIS OR AS *SEX AND THE CITY* SUGGESTS, 1990s NEW YORK.

Shake

DIFFICULTY: 🍸   **GLASS TYPE:** 🍸

REQUIRED: 60 ML CRANBERRY JUICE, 60 ML ORANGE JUICE, 60 ML LIME JUICE, ICE CUBES, MINT LEAVES FOR GARNISH

1 Place the cranberry, orange and lime juice in a cocktail shaker with ice and shake vigorously.

2 Strain over the martini glass.

3 Garnish with mint.

Zombie

HUNTER

THE ZOMBIE IS USUALLY RENOWNED
FOR ITS HIGH ALCOHOL CONTENT.
RENDERING IT VIRGIN OFFERS THE
OPPORTUNITY TO ENJOY ITS RICH
TROPICAL FLAVOURS, WHICH ARE
OFTEN OVERLOOKED IN FAVOUR OF
ITS STRENGTH. THIS ZOMBIE HUNTER
RECIPE CAN BE ENJOYED BY THE
GLASS, BUT IT'S ALSO PERFECT
TO SCALE UP FOR A PARTY PUNCH
BOWL – JUST MAKE SURE YOU LEAN
INTO THE TIKI VIBE WITH TROPICAL
DECORATIONS. TIKI NOT YOUR STYLE?
TAKE THE NAME SERIOUSLY AND SERVE
IT UP IN A SPOOKY SETTING FOR A
GREAT HALLOWEEN TREAT!

Shake

DIFFICULTY: 🍷   **GLASS TYPE:** 🥃

REQUIRED: 120 ML PINEAPPLE JUICE, 100 ML LIME JUICE, 120 ML SPARKLING GRAPE JUICE, DASH OF CINNAMON SYRUP, ICE CUBES, SLICE OF PINEAPPLE

1   Combine the pineapple, lime and grape juice with a generous dash of cinnamon syrup in your cocktail shaker and shake vigorously.

2   Strain over ice cubes into the glass.

3   Decorate with a slice of pineapple and a cocktail umbrella, if you have one.

THE MOST IMPORTANT THING FOR HAVING A PARTY IS THAT THE HOSTESS IS HAVING FUN.

INA GARTEN

Chocolate

PUDDING

THIS EXTREMELY INDULGENT CHOCOLATE PUDDING MOCKTAIL IS PERFECT FOR CHOCOHOLICS, AS A DECADENT EASTER TREAT OR AS AN ALTERNATIVE TO DESSERT AT YOUR NEXT DINNER PARTY. THE KEY TO MAKING THIS MOCKTAIL A CROWD-PLEASER IS IN THE UNIQUE RIM – FORGET THE SALT DIP OF THE NADA-RITA GLASS, THIS CHOCOLATE SPRINKLE RIM PUSHES THE TIPPLE OVER THE EDGE INTO UTTER INDULGENCE.

Shake

DIFFICULTY: 🍷🍷   **GLASS TYPE:** 🍸

REQUIRED: 50 G MILK CHOCOLATE, 130 ML MILK (DAIRY OR ALTERNATIVE), 35 ML CONDENSED MILK (OR ALTERNATIVE), 5 TBSP COCOA POWDER, ICE CUBES, 1 CREME EGG (OPTIONAL)

1 Microwave your chocolate on a plate in 20-second bursts until melted, then dip the rim of your glass and leave to dry.

2 Add the milk, condensed milk and cocoa powder to your cocktail shaker and shake vigorously.

3 Pour into the glass over ice.

4 For optional Easter garnish, wedge a creme egg onto the side of the glass by gently cutting a slit halfway up the egg.

Passion Star

MARTINI

A POPULAR DRINK AT NIGHTCLUBS, THE PORNSTAR MARTINI IS A SWEET, CHILLED COCKTAIL SERVED WITH PASSION FRUIT HALVES AND A SHOT OF PROSECCO. IT WAS INVENTED BY DOUGLAS ANKRAH, THE OWNER OF LONDON'S LAB BAR, WHO CLAIMS THAT HE GAVE THE DRINK ITS CONTROVERSIAL NAME BECAUSE IT WAS "SOMETHING THAT A PORNSTAR WOULD DRINK... PURE INDULGENCE, SEXY, FUN AND EVOCATIVE". THIS MOCKTAIL INCARNATION OF THE SEXY TIPPLE REPLACES THE PROSECCO WITH SPARKLING APPLE JUICE, SO IT STILL HAS THAT BUBBLY KICK.

Shake

DIFFICULTY: 🍸🍸　　**GLASS TYPE:** 🍸

REQUIRED: 150 ML SPARKLING APPLE JUICE, JUICE
OF 2 LIMES, 15 ML PASSION FRUIT SYRUP,
ICE CUBES, DASH OF VANILLA EXTRACT,
1 PASSION FRUIT

1 Add the sparkling apple juice, lime juice, syrup, ice
and a dash of vanilla extract to your cocktail shaker
and shake.

2 Halve the passion fruit, scoop out the seeds from
one half and add to the cocktail shaker.
Shake again.

3 Strain into a martini glass and garnish with the
remaining passion fruit half.

THERE IS SOMETHING URBANE, STYLISH, AND WORLDLY ABOUT OWNING A COCKTAIL SHAKER.

ROGER STONE

Pina

COL-NADA

IF YOU LIKE PINA COLADAS... HAVE WE GOT A RECIPE FOR YOU! THIS TROPICAL TREAT WITH RUM, PINEAPPLE AND COCONUT IS A SUMMER STAPLE WITH ORIGINS IN PUERTO RICO. THE NAME LITERALLY TRANSLATES FROM SPANISH AS "STRAINED PINEAPPLE", AND THE EARLIEST KNOWN STORY OF THE BEVERAGE IS OF A PUERTO RICAN PIRATE NAMED ROBERTO COFRESÍ, WHO USED THE COCKTAIL TO BOOST HIS CREW'S MORALE. IT HAS BEEN THE OFFICIAL DRINK OF PUERTO RICO SINCE 1978.

Shake

DIFFICULTY: 🍷   **GLASS TYPE:** 🍷

REQUIRED: 150 ML LEMONADE, 150 ML PINEAPPLE
JUICE, 60 ML COCONUT CREAM, ICE
CUBES, PINEAPPLE WEDGE

1 Combine the lemonade and pineapple juice with
the coconut cream in your cocktail shaker and
shake vigorously.

2 Strain over ice into your poco grande glass.

3 Garnish with a pineapple wedge and a cocktail
umbrella, if you have one.

MIMOS-NAH

A STAPLE TIPPLE FOR BOTTOMLESS BRUNCH ENTHUSIASTS, THE MIMOSA IS THE SEXIER AMERICAN COUSIN OF THE BRITISH "BUCKS FIZZ". ONE OF THE SIMPLER COCKTAILS, IT CONSISTS OF NOTHING MORE THAN CHAMPAGNE AND ORANGE JUICE – THE FRESHER THE BETTER. THE NAME "MIMOSA" COMES FROM THE MIMOSA PLANT, A BEAUTIFUL YELLOW FLOWER NATIVE TO AUSTRALIA. FOR THIS NON-ALCOHOLIC MIMOS-NAH, LEMONADE PROVIDES THE FIZZ AND A SPLASH OF GINGER ALE COMPENSATES FOR THE CHAMPAGNE'S BITE.

Stir

DIFFICULTY: 🍷   **GLASS TYPE:** 🥂

REQUIRED: 100 ML ORANGE JUICE, 100 ML LEMONADE, 100 ML GINGER ALE

1   Combine the orange juice, lemonade and ginger ale in your champagne flute. Bonus points if your orange juice is freshly squeezed.

2   Stir gently and drink immediately – don't let those bubbles go flat!

SUNDAY MORNING SPENT...
DRINKING SOME MIMOSAS
ALONE AND TALKING
UNTIL NOON. THAT WOULD
BE PRETTY AMAZING.
MARRIED COUPLES WITH
KIDS WILL UNDERSTAND.

DIERKS BENTLEY

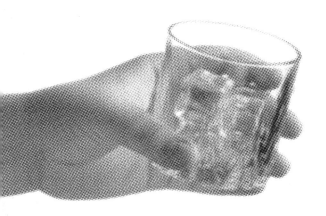

Booze-Free

BRAMBLE

CREATED IN LONDON'S FRED'S CLUB IN THE 1980s, THE BRAMBLE OFFERS THE VERY BRITISH FLAVOUR OF BLACKBERRIES, ACCOMPANIED BY GIN AND BERRY LIQUEUR. THIS FRESH MOCKTAIL INCARNATION HAS ALL THE TANGY FLAVOURS OF SUMMER BERRIES, AS WELL AS THAT DEEP PURPLE COLOUR, WITH JUNIPER SYRUP PROVIDING THE EDGE. WHY NOT MAKE THIS MOCKTAIL AN OCCASION BY FORAGING YOUR OWN BERRIES? THE BEST TIME TO DO SO IS MID-LATE SUMMER, WHEN BLACKBERRY BUSHES ARE LADEN WITH FRUIT.

Stir

DIFFICULTY: ♟ ♟   **GLASS TYPE:** ▮

REQUIRED: 3 DASHES OF SUGAR SYRUP, JUICE OF 1 LEMON, SMALL HANDFUL OF BLACKBERRIES, SMALL HANDFUL OF BASIL LEAVES, ICE CUBES, 150 ML SODA WATER

1 Stir together your sugar syrup and lemon juice until fully combined.

2 Add the berries and basil leaves (setting aside some berries and one leaf for garnish) and muddle until combined with the syrup and juice mixture.

3 Add ice cubes and top with soda water.

4 Garnish with some whole berries and a basil leaf.

Not-So

OLD FASHIONED

SOMETHING OF AN ACQUIRED, MATURE
TASTE AND PRESERVE OF MANY
A GENTLEMAN'S CLUB, THE OLD
FASHIONED COMBINES WHISKY WITH
BITTERS AND AN ORANGE GARNISH
FOR A STRONG COCKTAIL. REMOVING
THE ALCOHOL DOESN'T HAVE TO MEAN
LOSING THE REFINEMENT – THIS
MOCKTAIL VERSION TAKES A COLD
BREW APPROACH TO REPLACE THE
SOPHISTICATION OF WHISKY WITH
THE FLAVOURS OF HEAVILY STEEPED
TEA. MAKE YOUR DRINK EVEN MORE
AUTHENTIC BY POURING OVER A
LARGE, SINGLE, SPHERICAL ICE CUBE.

Stir

DIFFICULTY: 🍷 🍷   **GLASS TYPE:** ■

REQUIRED: BARLEY TEA (FOUND IN YOUR LOCAL ASIAN SUPERMARKET), 100 ML BOILING WATER, 1 TSP SUGAR, ORANGE SLICE, ICE CUBES, CHERRY AND ORANGE PEEL FOR GARNISH

1 Steep the tea in boiling water and leave to cool.

2 Muddle your sugar and orange slice in the bottom of the glass, then add ice cubes.

3 Add the tea and stir until the sugar dissolves.

4 Garnish with cherry and orange peel.

IF THERE'S ONE THING I'M
GOOD AT, IT'S GATHERING
PEOPLE TOGETHER TO
DO SOMETHING FUN.

DAVE GROHL

Virgin

STRAWBERRY DAIQUIRI

IF "REFRESHMENT" IS YOUR TOP
REQUIREMENT FROM A MOCKTAIL, THE
STRAWBERRY DAIQUIRI IS THE DRINK
OF YOUR DREAMS. LIGHT FLAVOURS
OF STRAWBERRY AND LIME COME
TOGETHER TO CREATE A SMOOTH
THIRST-QUENCHER WITH A LILT OF
CITRUS AND SWEETNESS. USUALLY
FORMULATED WITH RUM, THE DAIQUIRI
WAS NAMED AFTER A BEACH IN CUBA,
AND WAS SUPPOSEDLY INVENTED
BY AN AMERICAN MINING ENGINEER
WORKING AT THE NEARBY SANTIAGO
DE CUBA IRON MINE DURING THE
SPANISH—AMERICAN WAR AT THE END
OF THE NINETEENTH CENTURY.

Blend

DIFFICULTY: 🍸   **GLASS TYPE:** 🍸

REQUIRED: 150 G STRAWBERRIES (FROZEN OR FRESH) PLUS 1 FOR GARNISH, 100 ML ORANGE JUICE, JUICE OF 2 LIMES, 2 TBSP SUGAR, ICE CUBES

1   Prepare the strawberries, if using fresh berries, by removing stalks and leaves, saving one for garnish.

2   Place all ingredients in blender and blend at high speed until smooth.

3   Slice the strawberry garnish from the bottom to halfway up and slide onto the rim of the glass.

4   Decant the drink and enjoy.

Espress-no

MARTINI

FIND YOURSELF FLAGGING MIDWAY THROUGH ENTERTAINING? ENTER THE ESPRESSO MARTINI, A DELICIOUS COFFEE-BASED COCKTAIL WITH A POWERFUL PICK-ME-UP PUNCH, ALLEGEDLY CREATED BY BARTENDER DICK BRADSELL IN THE 1980s WHEN A YOUNG WOMAN ASKED FOR SOMETHING THAT WOULD "WAKE ME UP THEN F*** ME UP". THIS VIRGIN OPTION OFFERS ALL THE PEP AND NONE OF THE REGRET. THE KEY FOR A TRULY WINNING ESPRESSO MARTINI IS TO USE AS FINE A QUALITY ESPRESSO COFFEE AS YOUR BUDGET WILL ALLOW.

Shake

DIFFICULTY: 🍸   **GLASS TYPE:** Y

REQUIRED: 300 ML FRESHLY BREWED ESPRESSO
COFFEE (LEFT TO COOL), 5 ML VANILLA
SYRUP, 30 ML WATER, ICE CUBES,
3 COFFEE BEANS

1 Place all ingredients except the coffee beans into a cocktail shaker and shake vigorously.

2 Strain over the glass.

3 Garnish with three whole coffee beans.

DON'T GET STUCK IN A RUT WITH YOUR MARGARITA.

ANTONI POROWSKI

Not

TODDY

NOTHING CURES A SPLITTING HEADACHE OR STUFFY SINUSES QUITE LIKE A HOT TODDY. A STEAMING MUG OF THIS WARM COCKTAIL HAS BENEFITS BOTH MEDICINAL AND FLAVOURFUL WITH ITS MIX OF HONEY, HERBS AND SPICES. BUT THIS MOCKTAIL INCARNATION SHOULDN'T BE RESERVED FOR A STINKING COLD — MANY OF ITS INGREDIENTS HAVE GREAT IMMUNITY-BOOSTING QUALITIES, SO IT COULD ACTUALLY STOP YOU FROM GETTING SICK IN THE FIRST PLACE.

Stir

DIFFICULTY: ♟♟   GLASS TYPE: ▮

REQUIRED: 4 CM PEELED GINGER ROOT, 4 CM PEELED TURMERIC ROOT, 1 TSP GROUND CINNAMON, PINCH OF GROUND BLACK PEPPER, ORANGE ZEST, 300 ML HOT WATER, 1 TBSP OF HONEY, JUICE OF 1 LEMON, 1 CINNAMON STICK, ORANGE SLICES

1 Place all ingredients except the honey, lemon, cinnamon stick and orange slices in your glass and pour over the hot (not boiling) water.

2 Leave to infuse for a few minutes, then remove the roots.

3 Add the honey and lemon to taste.

4 Garnish with stick of cinnamon and orange slices.

Alcohol-Free

APEROL SPRITZ

YOU'D HAVE TO HAVE BEEN LIVING
UNDER A ROCK NOT TO CLOCK
THE EXPLOSION IN POPULARITY
OF THE HUMBLE APEROL SPRITZ
IN RECENT YEARS. SUMMERTIME
BRINGS WITH IT A HOST OF ORANGE
UMBRELLAS AND DEDICATED APEROL
BARS ACROSS MOST CITIES, AND
YOU CAN EVEN BUY THE WINNING
COMBO PREMIXED IN A CAN. FOR
THIS VIRGIN VERSION, MUDDLED
ORANGE PEEL OFFERS THE BITTER
NOTES OF ITS COCKTAIL COUSIN.

Stir

DIFFICULTY: 🍹   **GLASS TYPE:** ▪

REQUIRED: ORANGE PEEL, ICE CUBES, 150 ML ORANGE
JUICE, 100 ML SODA WATER, ORANGE SLICE

1 Muddle a single piece of orange peel at the bottom
of the glass. Add ice cubes, orange juice and top off
with soda water.

2 Slice up to the midway point of your orange slice,
and slide onto the rim of your glass.

3 Gently stir and enjoy.

I TRY TO GREET MY FRIENDS
WITH A DRINK IN MY HAND,
A WARM SMILE ON MY
FACE, AND GREAT MUSIC
IN THE BACKGROUND.

INA GARTEN

Side

N A H

SIDE CARS ARE A GREAT CHOICE
FOR THOSE WITH A DRIER PALETTE,
THOUGH THEY'RE AMONG THE MORE
CHALLENGING COCKTAILS TO CREATE
DUE TO THE CAREFUL BALANCE
REQUIRED BETWEEN THEIR SWEET
AND BITTER INGREDIENTS. IT'S
THOUGHT THAT THE RECIPE FIRST
EMERGED AFTER THE FIRST WORLD
WAR IN EITHER LONDON OR PARIS,
WHERE IT WAS NAMED AFTER THE
MODE OF TRANSPORT, WHICH WAS
EXTREMELY POPULAR AT THE TIME.
THE KEY TO THIS NON-ALCOHOLIC
SIDE NAH TAKE ON THE TIPPLE IS TO
REPLACE THE BOOZE WITH COLD TEA.

DIFFICULTY: ❚ ❚ ❚ GLASS TYPE: 🍸

REQUIRED: LOOSE LEAF LAPSANG SOUCHONG TEA,
100 ML BOILING WATER, JUICE OF 1 LEMON,
1 TSP MARMALADE, 1 TSP HONEY, ICE
CUBES, ORANGE SLICE AND PEEL
TO GARNISH

1 Steep the tea in boiling water, strain and allow to cool. Discard the leaves.

2 Put the tea water and lemon juice in your cocktail shaker with the marmalade and shake until the marmalade dissolves into the liquid.

3 Stir in the honey and shake again.

4 Strain into your glass over ice and garnish with the orange slice and peel.

Anna

BANANA

QUIRKY FLAVOUR COMBINATIONS
ARE AT THE HEART OF THIS MODERN
MOCKTAIL CONCEPT. DUE TO ITS
THICKNESS, BANANA IS RARELY
UTILISED IN COCKTAILS, BUT FOR
FANS OF A DRINK WITH A HEAVIER
BODY, IT'S A DELICIOUS ALTERNATIVE
TO A STANDARD TIKI DRINK. USE
A BLENDER TO ENSURE THAT THE
CONSISTENCY IS AS SMOOTH AS
POSSIBLE AND DOESN'T TAKE ON
THE HEAVINESS OF A SMOOTHIE.
GREAT AS A DESSERT ALTERNATIVE
AT YOUR NEXT DINNER PARTY!

Blend

DIFFICULTY: 🍷🍷   **GLASS TYPE:** ▮

REQUIRED: 2 BANANAS, 2 TBSP LIME JUICE, 120 ML COLD WATER, ICE CUBES, WHIPPED CREAM, LIME SLICE

1 Place all the ingredients except the cream and lime slice into blender and blend until smooth, adding water if it requires further thinning.

2 Pour directly into the glass without straining, and garnish with a dollop of whipped cream and lime slice.

MY FAVOURITE THING
IN THE WORLD IS TO
HAVE JUST A BIG DINNER
WITH FRIENDS.

LYKKE LI

Classic

MARTINI

PERHAPS THE COOLEST COCKTAIL AROUND, A MARTINI IS THE HEIGHT OF SOPHISTICATION, AS SHOWN THROUGH ITS MOST FAMOUS DRINKER, JAMES BOND. MADE WITH GIN AND VERMOUTH AND USUALLY GARNISHED WITH A SINGLE OLIVE, THE MARTINI WAS DESCRIBED BY THE WRITER H. L. MENCKEN AS "THE ONLY AMERICAN INVENTION AS PERFECT AS THE SONNET". A VIRGIN MARTINI BORROWS MORE FROM THE COCKTAIL'S STYLE THAN ITS FLAVOUR, BUT TO ADD A TOUCH OF GLAMOUR TO YOUR PARTY, IT'S WELL WORTH THE EFFORT.

Shake

DIFFICULTY: ♟

GLASS TYPE: Y

REQUIRED: 165 ML SODA WATER, DASH OF OLIVE
BRINE, 3 PITTED GREEN OLIVES

1 Combine the soda water and olive brine in a
cocktail shaker if you take your Martini shaken, or
straight in the glass if you favour stirred.

2 Spear your olives onto a cocktail stick and place in
the glass.

3 If you opted for shaken, pour your blend into the
glass. If stirred is your preference, use the cocktail
stick to blend the ingredients.

4 Enjoy fresh, to preserve the bubbles.

CONCLUSION

With so many options now in your mocktail armoury, you're ready to become a booze-free bartender extraordinaire. And now that you've read the rules, it's time to break them! The real fun of mocktail-making lies in experimentation and discovering new flavour combinations for your own bespoke virgin tipples. Whether you're stirring a classic Martini or getting creative blending an all-new Daiquiri combination, fun is at the heart of these cheeky grown-up soft drinks, so let your inner child run wild. Cheers!

Have you enjoyed this book? If so, find us on Facebook at **SUMMERSDALE PUBLISHERS**, on Twitter at **@SUMMERSDALE** and on Instagram at **@SUMMERSDALEBOOKS** and get in touch. We'd love to hear from you!

WWW.SUMMERSDALE.COM